MILHOUS I
Lord of San Clemente
Duke of Key Biscayne
Captain of Watergate

SUPERPEN

The Cartoons and Caricatures of Edward Sorel

Edited and Designed by
Lidia Ferrara

A Random House Book 🏠 *New York*

Dedication: For my mother

Copyright © 1978 by Edward Sorel
All rights reserved under International and Pan-American
Copyright Conventions. Published in the United States by
Random House, Inc., New York, and simultaneously
in Canada by Random House of Canada Limited, Toronto.
Library of Congress Cataloging in Publication Data
Sorel, Edward, 1929–
Superpen.
1.   American wit and humor, Pictorial.   I.   Title.
NC1429.S568A57   741.5'973   77–90236
ISBN 0–394–50002–4
2 4 6 8 9 7 5 3
First Edition
Grateful acknowledgment is made to the following for
permission to reprint previously published material:
American Heritage, Antioch Review 1970, Volume 30,
Number 2, *Atlantic Monthly, Esquire, Horizon,
Marie-Claire, New York Magazine, The New York Times,
Penthouse Magazine, Politicks, Screw Magazine, University
Review, The Village Voice,* and *The Washington Post.*

FOREWORD

For the past fifteen years I've been making cartoons that in one way or another suggest that America is educated by incompetents, governed by hypocrites, and ruled by the military-industrial complex. As a result of this anarchistic proselytizing, my alma mater has given me its highest award, the Senate has requested my art for permanent exhibition, and a wholly owned subsidiary of RCA has published this book.

Some decades you just can't do anything wrong.

But it was not always thus. When I first started hustling cartoons in the early sixties, only the most innocuous ideas ever found their way into a major periodical. The political ones had to go into underground newspapers like the *Realist* or into small-circulation magazines like *Monocle*, Victor Navasky's short-lived political humor magazine. It's hard to say how long things might have remained that way had not LBJ boarded that long escalator to Vietnam. But board it he did, and gave rise to a politically mordant Jules Feiffer in the *Village Voice*, to David Levine's devastating caricatures of everyone in power in the *New York Review of Books*, and to a whole bestiary of villains created by me for the California-based *Ramparts*. Suddenly outrage was more than permissible—it was fashionable.

By the late sixties I was doing a regular feature called "The Spokesman" for *Esquire* and another called "Unfamiliar Quotations" for the *Atlantic*. Then Clay Felker and Milton Glaser started *New York* magazine, and I signed on as a contributing editor. I turned out some of my best illustrations during this period, but almost all were in color and therefore could not be included in this collection. "Sorel's News Service" got off the ground about this time, too, and was syndicated by King Features for a year and a half; its demise after a (to my mind) not particularly vicious attack on our President reassured me that there was still a Middle America and that Middle America still had its limits. Then Felker bought the *Village Voice*, too, and offered me a third of page three to do with as I pleased each week. Unhampered by restrictions, suggestions, or editing, I had only to worry about my spelling and about how to compete with Jules Feiffer (page four).

Essentially my cartoons still reach comparatively few people. I am therefore doubly grateful for this book, and for the invaluable (if occasionally impractical) suggestions of my wife, Nancy, and such friends as Kirkpatrick Sale, Robert Levin, and Milton Newborn. A very special thanks goes to Lidia Ferrara.

—*Edward Sorel*

CARICATURES

Harry and Dick: Global Policeman

John Mitchell, before and after

Cornelia's little boy

Top: Robert Novak, Rowland Evans, and Stewart and Joseph Alsop; **bottom:** John Mitchell and Strom Thurmond; **right:** Robert Moses

The Emergence of the Third World

Peace Offensive

Vietnam, 1973

America, 1977

Tax Audit

Mild Recession

Pietà with Norman Vincent Peale and Billy Graham

Après moi le déluge

Watergate before . . . and after

Sisyphus

"I think the evidence as a whole, the new evidence as well as the old evidence, clearly exonerates the President of any involvement in the break-in, of any involvement in the I.T.T. and milk fund or impeachable offense, and I think the preponderance of evidence, all of it, is in favor of the President and exonerates him from any impeachable offense."—*Vice President Ford*

"He has his mother's deep moral integrity, and in this sense I would call him basically devout."—
Rev. Ezra Ellis, Paster of First Friends Meeting, Whittier, California

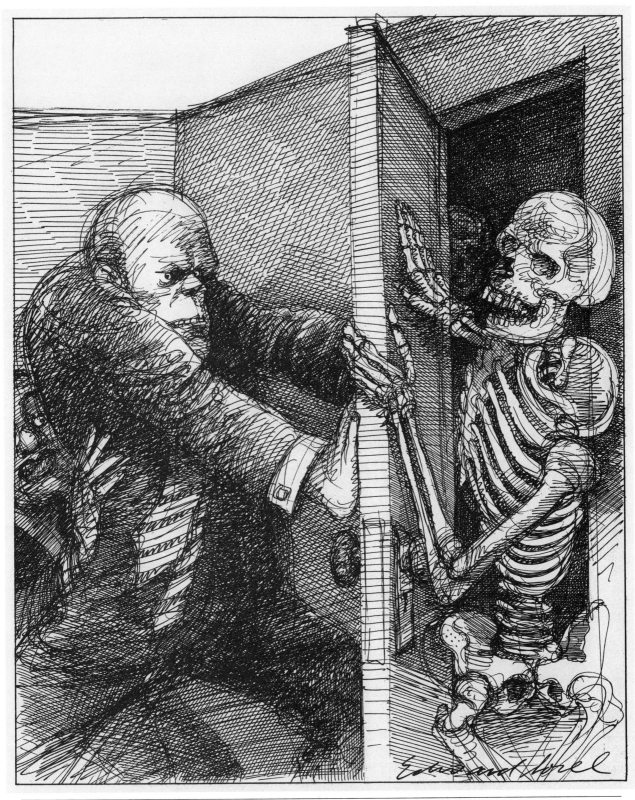

Spook Cover-Up Denied

Ron Nessen has denied that the White House was engaged in a "cover-up" of CIA assassination plots. "This President has been in office for ten months now," said the press secretary. "I think that is more than enough time for this blind, mindless, irrational suspicion and cynicism and distrust to evaporate."

Pedigree

San Clemente, California—In a recent conversation with a former member of his White House staff, Richard Nixon discussed grooming his daughter Julie for a career in politics, observing that "after all, she is both a Nixon and an Eisenhower."

Sic Transit Gloria

"Women's obsession with romance is a displacement of their longings for success."—*Gloria Steinem, New York Times Magazine, August 11, 1974*

Jackson cartoon: April 5, 1976

"We've had enough of being kicked around . . . We've been a soft touch for too long"—*Senator Henry Jackson (D), Boeing*

Oversight at the O.K. Corral

Press revelations about CIA–Howard Hughes salvage job, CIA involvement in assassination plots, and CIA links to organized crime have inspired Ronald Reagan to new heights of patriotic concern. "Freedom of speech and freedom of the press are wonderful," said the former governor, "but sometimes I think we shouldn't say something just because we have found it out." Mr. Reagan is a member of the blue-ribbon panel investigating the CIA.

The Ford Is My Shepherd

"Perhaps we as Christians failed to pray enough for Richard Nixon. Let us not make the same mistake in failing to pray for President Ford."—*Rev. Billy Graham*

What's This Guy Been Smoking?

When Jacob Javits accepted an invitation from Prince Saud al-Faisal to dine with him at Jidda on the shores of the Red Sea, there were the inevitable raised eyebrows. When, subsequently, Javits continued to meet socially with the Saudi Arabian foreign minister, some of the senator's Jewish constituents "expressed their concern." Questioned about this, Javits responded: "The Jewish people are convinced that I cannot be corrupted."

Buckley Contemplating the Head of Ford

"People who have experienced Gerald Ford at close quarters know that he is a man of nimble intelligence who quickly understands the dimensions of a problem."—*William Buckley*

Great Ideas of Pro-Western Man (Blood, Sweat, and Cheers Division)

"Our plans must include efforts to maintain economic growth. We may also have to consider ways of adapting what the Europeans call 'industrial democracy' to our own social conditions, creating mechanisms for greater social participation in economic decision-making. That will surely strengthen, rather than weaken, our democracy. I also believe that a call to the nation to sacrifice would contribute a great deal to the restoration of optimism, for sacrifice generates optimism."—*Zbigniew Brzezinski*

Dr. Jake and Mr. Hyde

Jacob Javits's sudden changes of face have long been a concern to his friends and loved ones. Last week he did it again. After his staff had prepared a press release announcing his opposition to further military aid to Cambodia, the senator changed his mind and joined with the 4–3 majority in the Foreign Relations Committee to continue American aid. He explained his changed attitude with: "I don't want to be the one who gave Cambodia the last push to a bloodbath."

The Great Waltz

"There is nothing wicked about being the party of business."—*Senator Jacob Javits*

Chase Has a Friend at the Federal Reserve

When Consumer Action sought to list the range of interest rates charged by banks in San Francisco, they were denied the information by the Federal Reserve Board. Arthur Burns, chairman of the board, admitted that such information "is potentially very useful to consumers" but nevertheless refused to supply the data on the grounds it was "confidential." This is the same Arthur Burns who, while serving Richard Nixon, forwarded to the IRS the names of certain peace advocates for investigation.

Truth Is Booty, Booty Is Truth

"There is already an inclination to trust the Veep-designate precisely because he is rich. 'When somebody is one of the wealthiest men in the world,' said Rep. John Rhodes of Arizona, the Republican leader in the house, 'he's got so much money there would be no point in cheating.'"

". . . And Then I Wrote . . ."

"The first patches of blue in the gray wintery sky of steep inflation have begun to appear."—*Secretary of the Treasury William Simon, New York Times, March 11*

Theodore White Working On New Nixon Portrait

New York, Sept. 25—Atheneum in conjunction with Reader's Digest Press has paid Theodore White an advance of $150,000 to write *The Nixon Story.* The forthcoming book will be about "the abuse of power" and will, presumably, be quite different from his *The Making of the President 1972,* in which Mr. Nixon was depicted as wise, commanding and judicious. Questioned about that book and his flattering portrait of the former President, Mr. White defended himself: "I was lied to."

Making the World Safe for Hypocrisy

"Our marvelous city is being victimized by a small group of promoters who care nothing about human values, only about dollars."—*Cardinal Cooke, in his Declaration of War on Pornography, April 5, 1977*

Questions Without Answers

Cardinal Cooke visited Vietnam and told American soldiers stationed there: "You are friends of Christ by the fact that you come over here." Question: Would the Cardinal have taken a less benevolent attitude had our soldiers been firing at fetuses instead of men?

Money (Short) Changer in the Temple

On New Year's Day, Pope Paul urged a lower-middle-class congregation in Rome to disdain cunning and "shun a Mafia-style mentality." On January 31, however, the Vatican admitted that Sicilian-born financier Michele Sindona (now a fugitive from justice) had assisted the Church in several financial transactions. It further conceded that when Mr. Sindona's financial empire collapsed, the Institute for Works of Religion (commonly referred to as the "Vatican Bank") suffered "limited" financial losses. These "limited" losses are estimated to be $55 million.

Lights . . . Chimera . . . Action

When the Vatican attacked Hollywood for grinding out movies about Satan for no purpose other than fast profits, a reply from the movie capital was inevitable. It came, not surprisingly, from 20th Century-Fox, producers of *The Omen*: "They must admit that the devil can be alive and well on planet Earth, and if so, isn't it important to gather our religious strength to ward off this evil? The best way to do that is to have an informed public."

Great Ideas of Western Man

"The revisionist historians are having a field day now, but in the postwar era, the United States has been at its best when confronted by serious trouble and at its worst when it was sweet-talked into dreams of a phony perpetual peace."—*James Reston, May 15, 1975*

"War alone brings up to its highest tension all human energy and puts the stamp of nobility upon the peoples who have the courage to face it."—*Benito Mussolini, 1935*

Fear of Blocking (Or, The Fart Is a Lonely Hunter)

In *Loveroot*, Erica Jong's collection of poems, is one entitled "Unblocked." It describes how she recovered from Writer's Block when "you appeared, seized me quite suddenly . . . paper clipped by nipples," and "I felt that fatal spasm of love & lost my dinner. I felt that hunger for you & I had diarrhea . . . but the Muse winged over the toilet . . . that fateful night & now I am sick again & now can write."

Prude of the Week

"There's nothing wrong with going to bed with somebody of your own sex. I think everybody's bisexual to a certain degree. I don't think it's just me. It's not a bad thing to be. I think you're bisexual. I think everybody is . . . I mean, who cares! I just think people should be very free with sex—they should draw the line at goats."—*Elton John, from an interview in* Rolling Stone

News from the World of Art (Function Follows Form Division)

Although a sculpture by Claes Oldenburg usually sells for around $50,000, a recent creation, *Toast,* which is carved out of marble, is said to be going for $80,000. One explanation for this price jump was offered in *People* magazine, which interviewed Mr. Oldenburg. *"Toast,"* he says, "can double as a sundial."

I Thought He Was On Our Side

While spokesmen for Con Edison continue to explain away their company's responsibility for the blackout, Charles Luce, chairman of the utility company, offered the definitive explanation: "It appears it was an act of God."

Sail on, O Ship of State

A new congressional study* has found that the average tax rate paid by the largest 102 corporations in the United States is significantly smaller than those paid by smaller companies. The Ford Motor Company, with a corporate profit of $300 million in 1974, paid no taxes at all that year. In fact, it received more than $50 million in tax credits, which it can deduct in future years. Other corporations paying no taxes were American Electric Power, Honeywell, Allstate Insurance, Lockheed, Eastern Airlines, and American Airlines. Had these and other corporations paid the base corporate profit rate in 1974, their tax revenues would have totaled in the billions. *Congressional Joint Committee on Internal Revenue Taxation*

"Nixon has sex appeal—he's slim and suntanned and . . . well, he's just sexy, that's all. And I call that charming."
—*Barbara Walters*

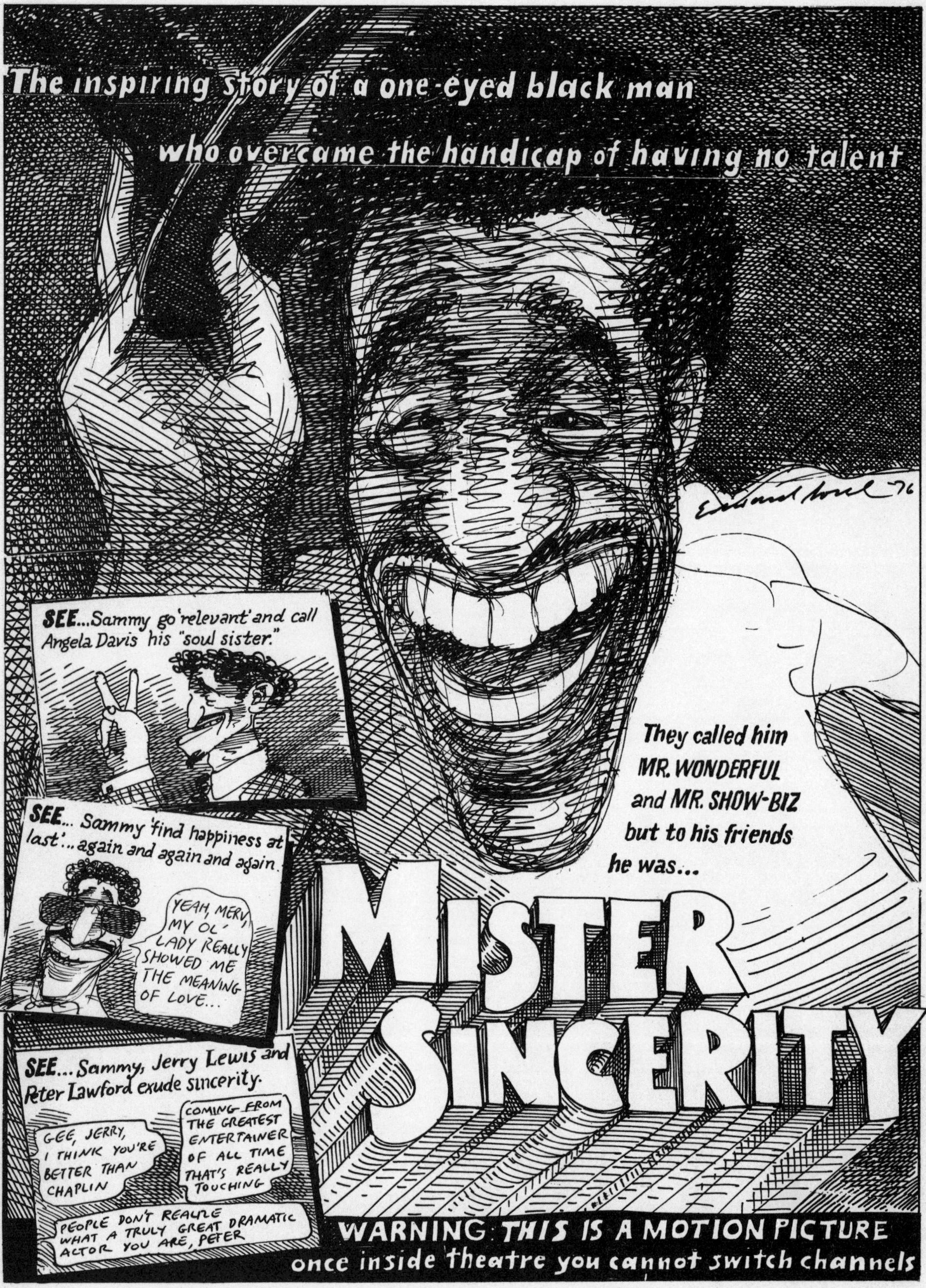
The inspiring story of a one-eyed black man
who overcame the handicap of having no talent
SEE...Sammy go 'relevant' and call Angela Davis his "soul sister."
SEE... Sammy 'find happiness at last'... again and again and again.
YEAH, MERV, MY OL' LADY REALLY SHOWED ME THE MEANING OF LOVE...
SEE... Sammy, Jerry Lewis and Peter Lawford exude sincerity.
GEE, JERRY, I THINK YOU'RE BETTER THAN CHAPLIN
COMING FROM THE GREATEST ENTERTAINER OF ALL TIME THAT'S REALLY TOUCHING
PEOPLE DON'T REALIZE WHAT A TRULY GREAT DRAMATIC ACTOR YOU ARE, PETER
They called him MR. WONDERFUL and MR. SHOW-BIZ but to his friends he was...
MISTER SINCERITY
WARNING: THIS IS A MOTION PICTURE
once inside theatre you cannot switch channels

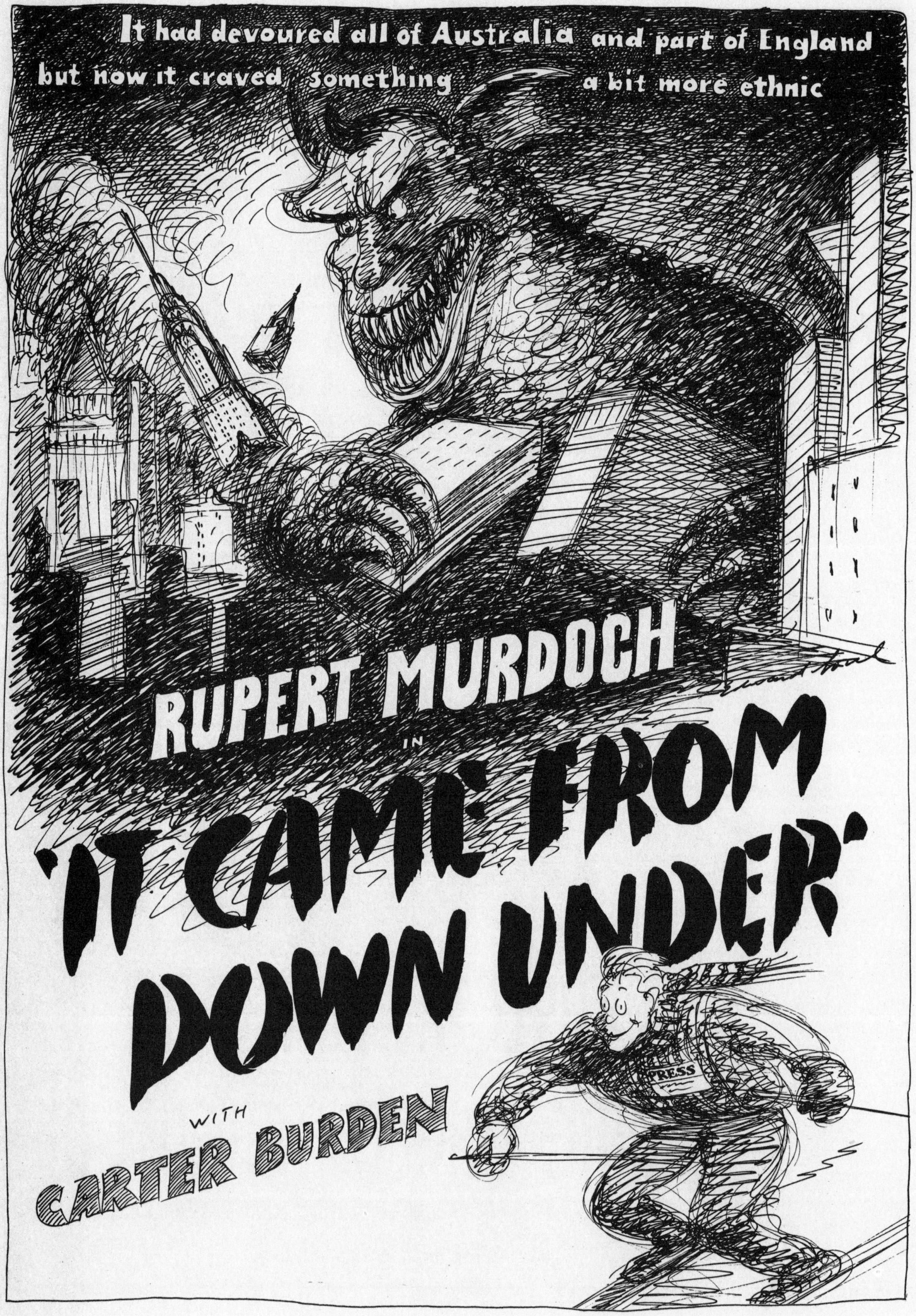
It had devoured all of Australia and part of England
but now it craved something a bit more ethnic
RUPERT MURDOCH
IN
'IT CAME FROM DOWN UNDER'
WITH
CARTER BURDEN
PRESS

NOT TO THE... NOT TO THE BEST OF MY RECOLLECTION... NOT TO THE BEST OF MY RECOLLECTION~ NOT TO THE...
BY GOD! I THINK HE'S GOT IT! BY JOVE, HE'S GOT IT!
The screen thunders to a spectacular thud when
SON of FRANKENSTEIN MEETS SON of GOD
FINAL WEEK

EXTREMISM IN DEFENSE OF VICE IS SOMETIMES VIRTUE

Henry Kissinger on the road

Rex Reed at the movies

John Wayne

Woody Allen

Frank Sinatra

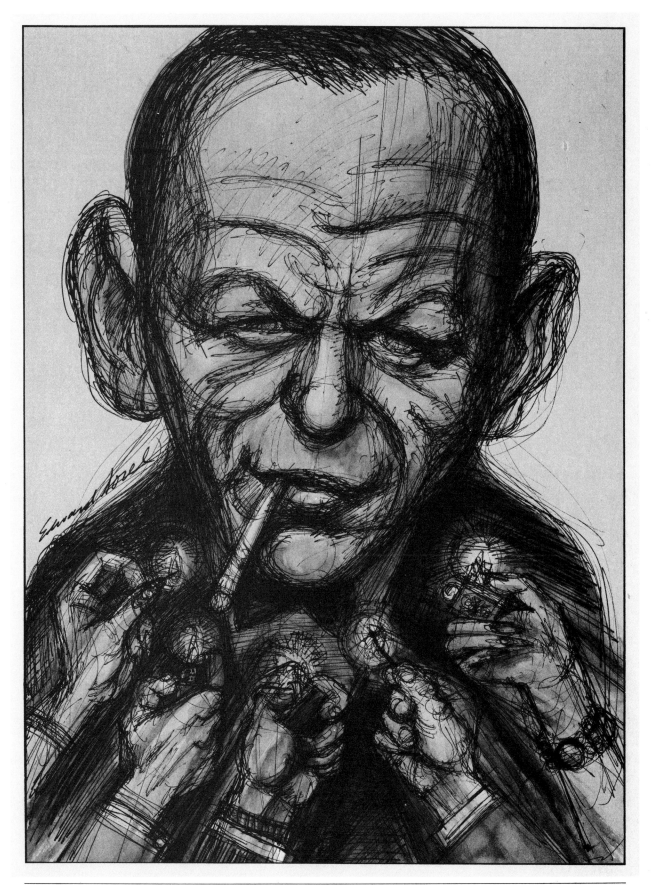

. . . and friends

Joe DiMaggio

Babe Ruth

Left to right: Ellis, Master, Johnson, Van de Velde, Kensey, Freud.

Erasmus (after Holbein)

Ben Jonson

Johann Sebastian Bach

Lucky Lindy

Buffalo Bill

The Making of <u>Gone with the Wind</u>. "Meet Your Scarlett O'Hara!"

Top left: Margaret Mitchell; **top right:** Ashley; **bottom left:** Scarlett; **bottom right:** Rhett

Top left: Amelia Jerks Bloomer; **top right:** Duns Scotus; **bottom left:** Luigi Galvani; **bottom right:** James Watt

Robert Peale (Bobby)

Top left: Jean Martinet; **top right:** Rudolph Diesel; **bottom left:** Marquis de Sade; **bottom right:** Louis-Jacques-Mandé Daguerre

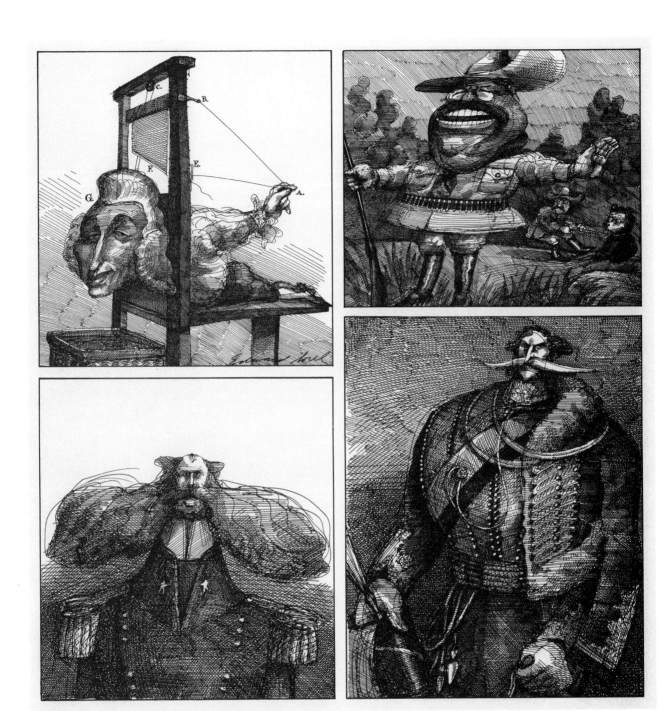

Top left: Dr. Joseph Ignace Guillotin; **top right:** Theodore Roosevelt; **bottom left:** Ambrose Burnside; **bottom right:** Earl of Cardigan

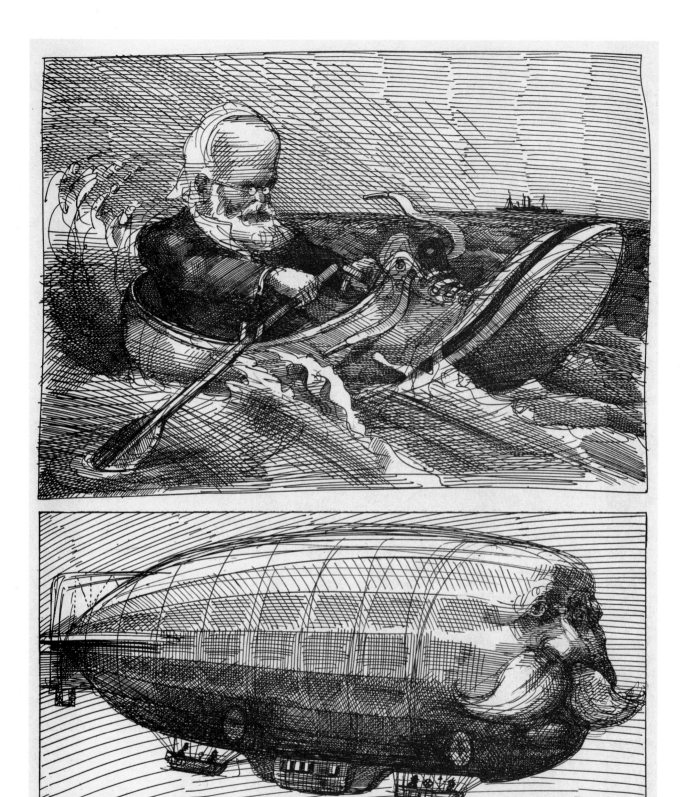

Top: Samuel Plimsoll; **bottom:** Count Ferdinand von Zeppelin

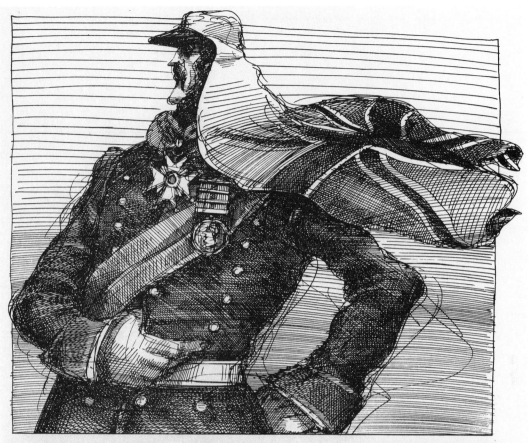

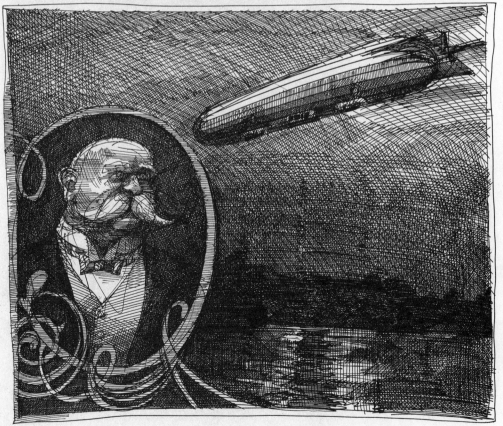

Top: Henry Havelock; **bottom:** Count Ferdinand von Zeppelin

Monumental Folly by Donald Barthelme

Progress

[Left] Progress is wonderful, and continues to become more wonderful with each passing fiscal year. Progress is the basic American idea, and no country's Progress exceeds our own, by executive order. Progress is often the target of cheap sneers by sour yawpers, but even a sour yawper can ascend dark stairs holding a silver candlestick in his hand. If Progress continues to butter up the quality of life at the present rate, everyone will be unbearably happy by breakfast, 1999. Huzzah!

Disaster

[Above] Disaster is delicious. A good sack o' woe, budgeted at $6 million, will deliver 177 thrills and 22 *frissons* per hour. These elegant productions, from which all skin, bone, and gristle have been removed for easy intake, have a moral dimension, too. They vaguely remind you of fate, or something, the haunting contingency of human life, or something. Mostly they take your mind off your life, that ridiculous enterprise, and put your mind on someone else who is actually *on fire*. Well, you're better off than that dummy, aren't you? Meanwhile, the army ants of capitalism are chewing off your shoes.

The Loophole

[Left] The Loophole is to the twentieth century what the frontier was to the nineteenth—a way out, a psychological fire escape. Loopholes, however, are not for everyone. They are hidden, like Easter eggs, and can only be found with the assistance of highly paid counsel. This monument is suitable for corporate plazas and also looks very handsome atop grain elevators.

Valium

[Above] Valium is what keeps airplanes in the air, cars on the highways, and the furnace rattling. These functions are often mistakenly attributed to Petroleum, but America knows better. In a time when ever more gruesome Revelations daily fritter the nerves, it is reassuring to note that domestic reserves are estimated at two million barrels a day of yellows and three million barrels a day of the 10 mg., or blues.

Nostalgia

In Bicentennial America, yesterday is terrific. Instead of yearning forwardly, which makes more sense in terms of the possible, we yearn backwardly, and who cares for "sense" anyhow! Gazing at a pile of old knickers, or an old duffel bag with our serial number stenciled on it, or an old cracked putter, we are suffused with a nameless emotion, which is called Golf. (We used to carry our clubs in the duffel bag, and if you think we weren't laughed at, you are wrong.) This monument is specially designed for closets, attics, and abandoned movie houses.

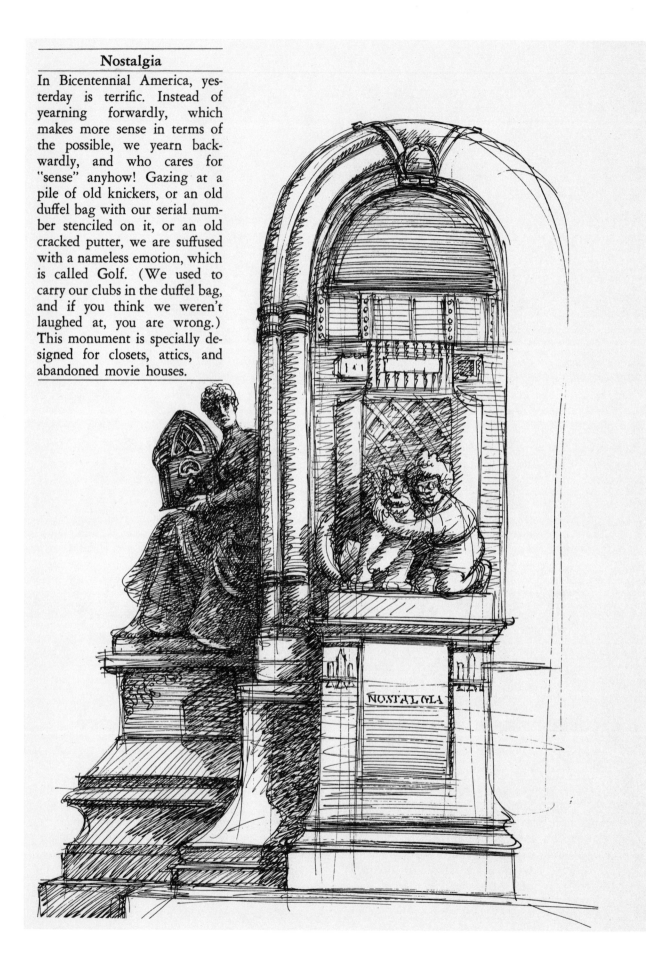

Divorce

Divorce is good in other countries, but nowhere is it as good as it is in our own—the sacred Elmer's glue which cements the social fabric. Without the sacrament of Divorce, who would be silly enough to get married? Nobody, except for people who don't care one way or another, the 15 percent of the population who are always, in America, "undecided," those clunks. What darkens the future of Divorce in America is the profession of law, which can make the whole process very unpleasant. It might not be a bad thing if jurisdiction were taken away from lawyers and given instead to plumbers. Plumbers know all about joining and unjoining and are slightly cheaper.

CARTOONS

President Nixon informs Gerald Ford he is going to nominate him for Vice President.

DECEMBER 13, 1973

NOVEMBER 1973

The Hippocratic Oaths

"First the <u>Pietà</u>, then <u>The Night Watch</u>, and now this."

...SO THE QUESTION AMERICANS MUST ASK THEMSELVES IS THIS: IF WASHINGTON COULD AFFORD TO SUPPORT ORGANIZED CORRUPTION IN VIETNAM WHY CAN'T IT SUPPORT ORGANIZED CORRUPTION IN NEW YORK?

NOVEMBER 1975

SEPTEMBER 8, 1975

WHEN WE SENT SPUTNIK INTO ORBIT IT CAME AS A COMPLETE SURPRISE TO THE C.I.A.. WE SOON REALIZED THAT ALMOST **EVERYTHING** CAME AS A SURPRISE TO THE C.I.A..

THE SUEZ INVASION TOOK THEM UNAWARE ... THE HUNGARIAN UPRISING, THE YOM KIPPUR WAR, OUR "LIBERATION" OF PRAGUE, THE PORTUGUESE REVOLUTION, THE FALL OF THE GREEK JUNTA, THE THREE BIGGEST COMMUNIST OFFENSIVES IN VIETNAM ... ALL CAME AS A SHOCK TO THE C.I.A.!

ASIDE FROM THEIR INCOMPETENCE WE NOTED THAT THE COST OF FINANCING C.I.A. ACTIVITIES WAS SO STAGGERING THAT IT WAS BEGINNING TO PUT A REAL STRAIN ON THE U.S. ECONOMY!!

WE HOPED THAT IF THE U.S. CONTINUED TO FUND THE CIA AT CURRENT LEVELS, THERE WOULD BE A COMPLETE ECONOMIC COLLAPSE BY 1978!! BUT *NOW* THERE ARE CERTAIN ELEMENTS IN AMERICA THAT ARE DEMANDING AN **END** TO THE C.I.A.!

DAMNED HOTHEAD LEFTWINGERS...

MARCH 1978

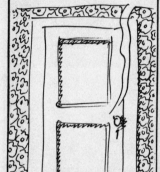

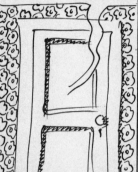

SEPTEMBER 26, 1977

SEPTEMBER 12, 1977

FEBRUARY 16, 1976

The Blackcoats Are Coming

As the United States approaches its two hundredth birthday, an army of churchmen are planning Bicentennial celebrations. The first of these programs, according to *Variety*, will come from Billy Graham. The Walter F. Bennett advertising agency has announced that the evangelist will do a half-hour "patriotic" television special on New Year's Eve.

Rumor of the Week

Friends of the late Aristotle Onassis say his marriage to Jacqueline Kennedy became strained after he gave her a set of Teflonware for their anniversary.

Rumor of the Week

A concerted campaign by a small but militant minority in the Gay Activist Alliance may soon be crowned with success. Unconfirmed reports from City Hall say the mayor is about to bow to their demands for the creation of an "S&M Pride Day." Leaders in the S&M community will be invited to the proclamation-signing ceremonies.

Rumor of the Week

Informed Washington sources report that the White House has engaged Walter Keane to paint the official portrait of President Ford.

TO PROTECT US FROM PROFIT-MAD UTILITIES, THE GOVERNMENT CREATED THE PUBLIC SERVICE COMMISSION...

...AND APPOINTED TO THIS COMMISSION MEN WHO WOULD GIVE THE UTILITIES EVERYTHING THEY ASKED FOR

TO PROTECT US FROM CRIMINALS THE GOVERNMENT CREATED THE FEDERAL BUREAU OF INVESTIGATION...

...AND APPOINTED TO THIS BUREAU MEN WHO BURGLED, BLACKMAILED AND PLANTED FALSE EVIDENCE

TO PROTECT US FROM BEING INVADED BY A BLOODTHIRSTY, RAPACIOUS, INHUMAN ENEMY THE GOVERNMENT CREATED THE PENTAGON...

...WHICH HAS SOLD OUR NEWEST RADAR COMPUTER TO BOTH RUSSIA AND CHINA!

WE HAD TO DO IT... WE KEPT TELLIN' YOU THAT THEY WERE CATCHIN' UP WITH US BUT YOU WOULDN'T BELIEVE US!

DECEMBER 20, 1976

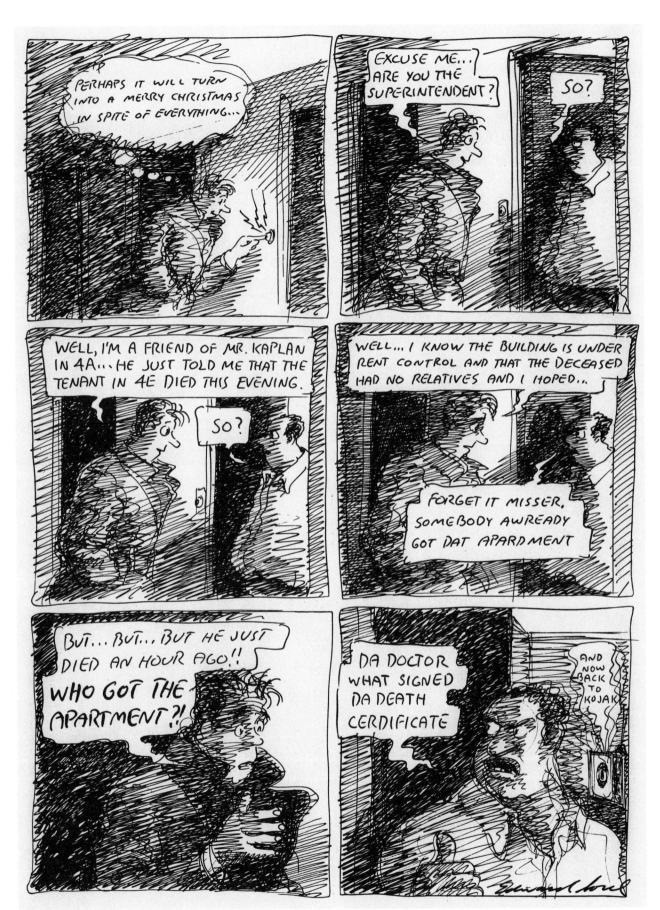

In an interview with Bill Moyers, Hubert Humphrey blamed Nguyen Van Thieu for sabotaging the 1968 Paris peace talks, referring to Thieu as "that no-good so-and-so." In March 1971, however, Mr. Humphrey was concerned about President Nixon withdrawing from Vietnam too precipitously: "I would have been proceeding that way, but a little more carefully. We have to be careful not to let Thieu collapse."

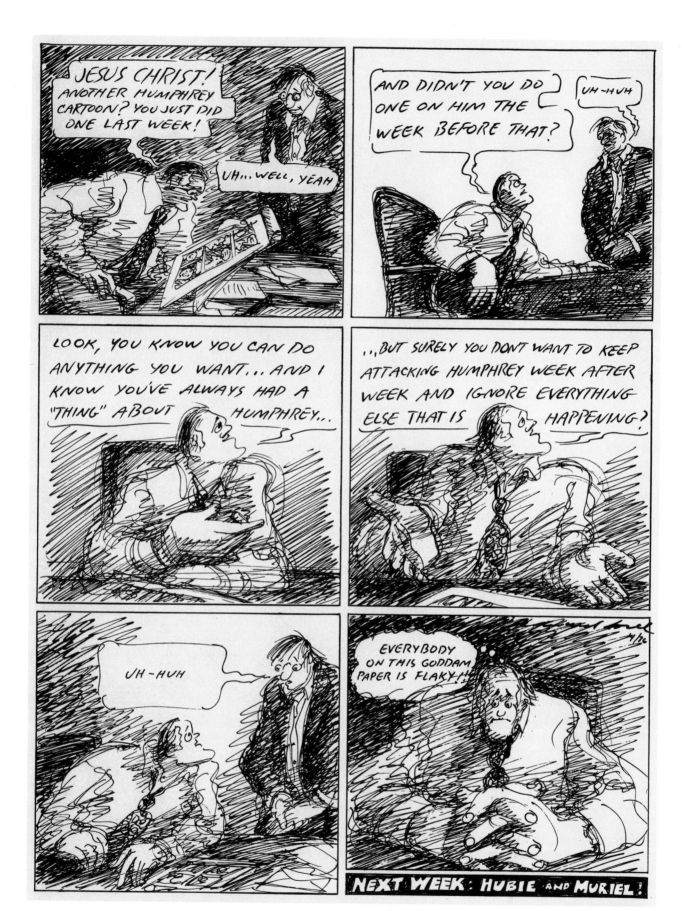

MAY 10, 1976

MAY 17, 1976

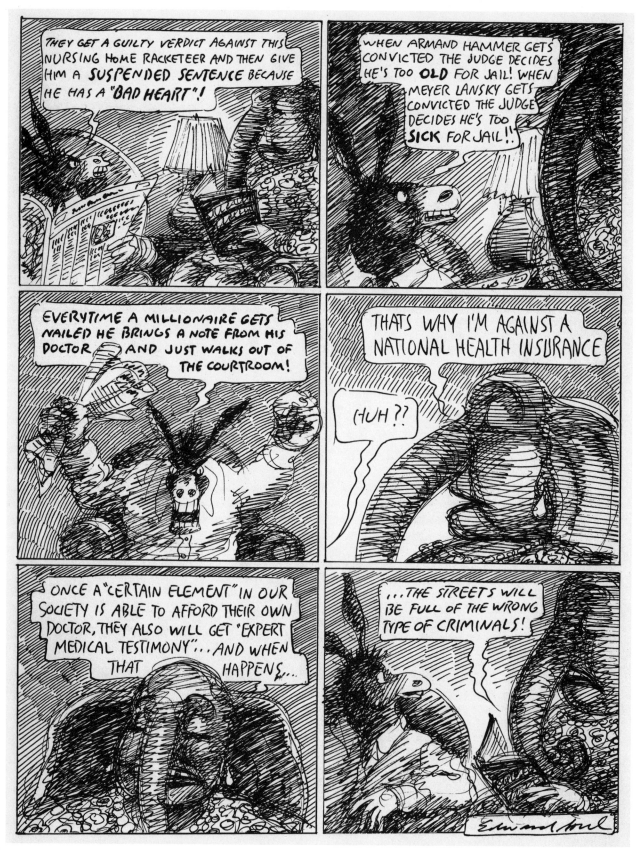

JUNE 7, 1976

JUNE 14, 1976

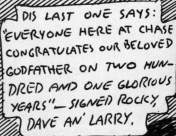

The Ozone Park branch of "Right to Life" learns that capital punishment has been declared constitutional.

JULY 2, 1976

"... and so as we go forward in the months ahead, let us take heart in the knowledge that in these United States there is nothing ... I repeat ... nothing that can stop an idea whose time has passed."

"No, this is Ways and Means. You want Defense down the hall."

JANUARY 1977

"Oh, you missed it! Mr. Mailer just gave a brilliant analysis of what's wrong with American writers."

" . . . and I've always been careful about my diet. In fact, without make-up I weigh exactly what I did when I made *Flying Down to Rio*."

"IT'S INCONCEIVABLE TO ME THAT ANYONE WOULD THINK HE COULD DO THIS JOB, THE PRESIDENCY, IF HE COULDN'T CALL ON GOD FOR HELP AND HAVE FAITH THAT HE'D BE GRANTED THAT HELP."
— TIME 5/17/76

I NEVER ACTUALLY SPOKE TO GOD BUT ONCE, WHEN I HIT MY HEAD GETTING OFF A PLANE, I THINK I SAW HIM. HE WAS VERY NICE.

WHITE HOUSE PRAYER BREAKFASTS ARE NOT ENOUGH...WE MUST BRING GOD HIMSELF INTO GOVERNMENT, PREFERABLY IN A HIGH CABINET POST.

THANKS TO MY DOCTRINE OF "LOWER EXPECTATIONS" MY FIRST MEETING WITH GOD WAS NOT A DISAPPOINTMENT.

NU? GO FIGURE IT!? THE DEVIL GETS H.L. MENCKEN, GEORGE BERNARD SHAW, SAM CLEMENS, BILLIE HOLIDAY, GERSHWIN, PORTER, SCHUBERT...AND...AND I...I KEEP GETTING DRECK LIKE THIS!!!

MAY 24, 1976

NOVEMBER 22, 1976

"You know, last night I made it with a 12-year-old, but like, man, she had the body of a 9-year-old."

Rumor of the Week

In its desperate search for additional revenues, the City Council is considering a measure that would legalize bribes to city officials in order to place a 10 percent tax on all such gratuities.

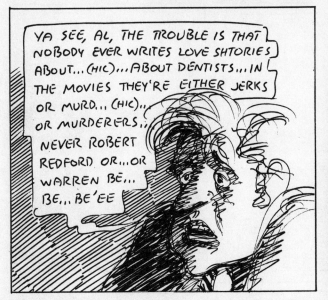

AUGUST 29, 1977

JULY 11, 1977

About the Author

A contributor to virtually every major American magazine, EDWARD SOREL is also the author of *How to Be President, Moon Missing* and *Making the World Safe for Hypocrisy*. He was born in New York City in 1929 and was a co-founder of The Push Pin Studio. He has exhibited at the Louvre, and appears weekly in the *Village Voice*. He was awarded Cooper Union's Augustus St. Gaudens Medal in 1973.